J 743.6
Scer

* dewey # and spine label
are correct

Art Works™ Drawing Dinosaurs and other prehistoric Animals

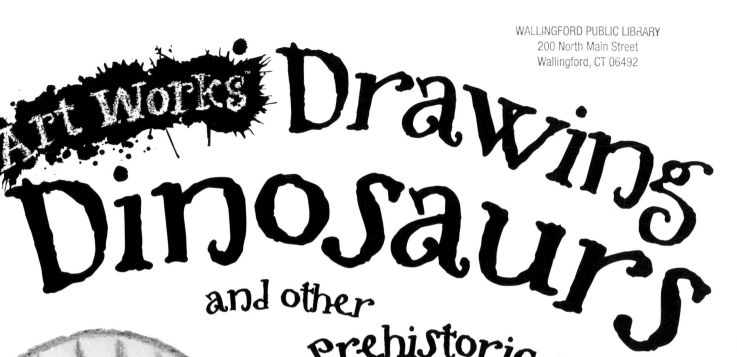

carolyn Scrace

A⁺
Smart Apple Media

Author:
Carolyn Scrace graduated from Brighton College of Art, England, after studying design and illustration. Since then she has worked in animation, advertising, and children's publishing. She has a special interest in natural history and has written many books on the subject, including *Lion Journal*, and *Gorilla Journal* in the *Animal Journal* series.

How to use this book:

Follow the easy, numbered instructions. Simple step-by-step stages enable budding young artists to create their own amazing drawings.

What you will need:

1. Paper to draw on.
2. Wax crayons for drawing.
3. Felt-tip pens to color in your drawings.

Published by Smart Apple Media,
an imprint of Black Rabbit Books
P.O. Box 3263, Mankato, Minnesota 56002
www.blackrabbitbooks.com

Published by arrangement with
The Salariya Book Company Ltd

Cataloging-in-Publication Data is available from the Library of Congress

Printed in the United States
At Corporate Graphics,
North Mankato, Minnesota

9 8 7 6 5 4 3 2 1

ISBN: 978-1-62588-344-5

Contents

 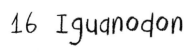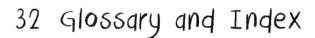

Tyrannosaurus

(Tie-ran-oh-sore-us)

1 A Tyrannosaurus needs a head,

2 ...a body,

3 ...a neck,

4 ...two strong legs,

5 ...two tiny arms and hands,

6 ...and a tail! Now draw in an eye, nose, and mouth.

Draw in eye ridges
(two bumps) on top
of Tyrannosaurus's head.

Eye ridge

Draw in sharp
pointed teeth
and finish his eye.

Color in with
felt-tip pens.

Triceratops

(Tri-serra-tops)

1 A Triceratops needs a head,

2 ...a body,

3 ...four strong legs,

4 ...a tail,

Neck frill

5 ...a neck frill,

6 ...and two horns on his head. Add a horn to his snout.

6

Draw a pattern around the edge of Triceratops's frill. Now draw in his eyes, beak, and mouth.

Color in with felt-tip pens.

Beak

Stegosaurus

(Steg-oh-sore-us)

1 A Stegosaurus needs a body,

2 ...a little head,

3 ...a neck,

4 ...four stumpy legs,

5 ...a tail,

6 ...and big spikes along her body!

8

Add spots. Draw in Stegosaurus's eyes, nose, and mouth.

Color in with felt-tip pens.

Diplodocus

(Dip-lo-dock-us)

1 A Diplodocus needs a body,

2 ...a long neck,

3 ...a small head,

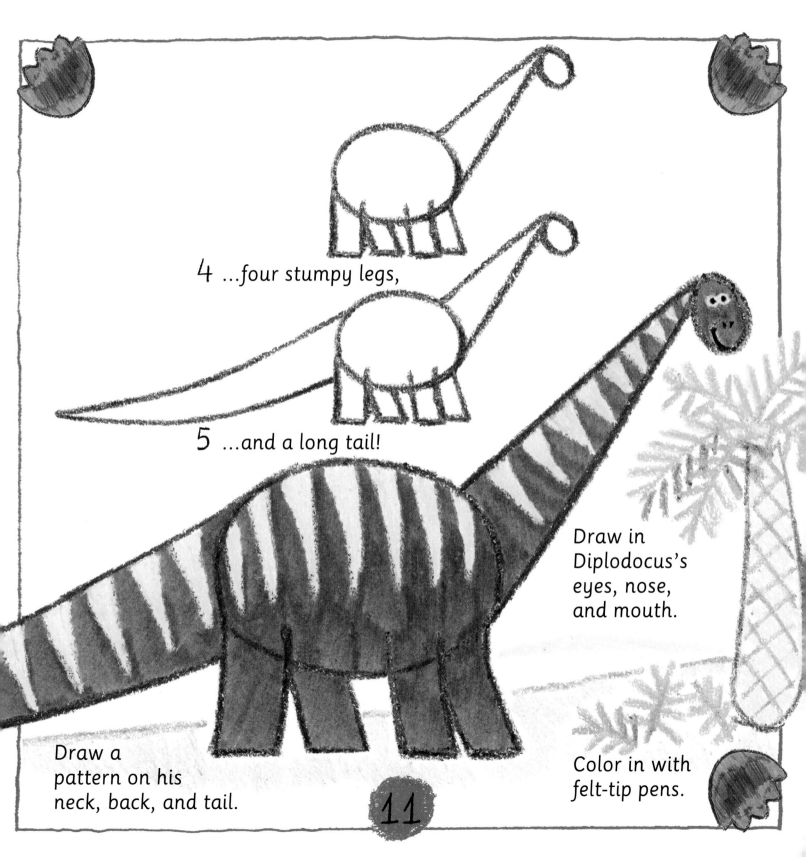

4 ...four stumpy legs,

5 ...and a long tail!

Draw in Diplodocus's eyes, nose, and mouth.

Draw a pattern on his neck, back, and tail.

Color in with felt-tip pens.

Plateosaurus

(Plat-ee-oh-sore-us)

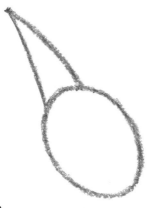

1 A Plateosaurus needs a body,

2 ...a neck,

3 ...a head,

4 ...two legs and feet,

5 ...two arms and hands,

6 ...and a big tail!

12

Draw in Plateosaurus's
eyes, nose, and mouth.

Then add spots to his
neck, body, leg, and tail.

Color in with
felt-tip pens.

13

Parasaurolophus

(Pa-ra-sore-rol-off-us)

1 A Parasaurolophus needs a body,

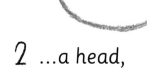

2 ...a head,

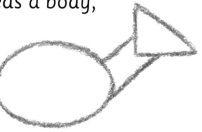

3 ...a neck,

4 ...two strong legs,

Head crest

5 ...two arms and hands,

6 ...and a tail and long head crest!

14

Draw in Parasaurolophus's eye, nose, and mouth.

Now draw stripes on his body, arms, and legs.

Color in with felt-tip pens.

15

Iguanodon

(Ig-wa-noh-don)

1 An Iguanodon needs a body,

2 ...a head,

3 ...a neck,

Thumb spikes

4 ...two sturdy legs,

5 ...two arms, two hands with thumb spikes,

6 ...and a tail!

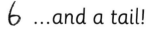

16

Draw in Iguanodon's
eyes, mouth, and fingers.

Draw a jagged
pattern on her body.

Crayon in iguanodon's
thumb spikes and nose.

Color in with
felt-tip pens.

Corythosaurus

(Koh-rith-oh-sore-us)

1 A Corythosaurus needs a body,

2 ...a head,

3 ...a neck,

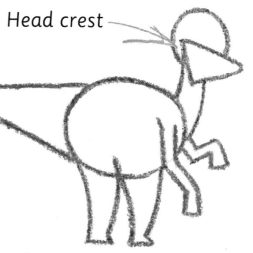

Head crest

4 ...two legs,

5 ...two arms,

6 ...and a tail! Now draw in his round head crest.

Draw in his eyes,
nose, and mouth.

Draw a wavy pattern
along Corythosaurus's
back and tail.

Color in with
felt-tip pens.

19

Ankylosaurus

(An-kie-loh-sore-us)

1 An Ankylosaurus needs a head,

2 ...a body,

3 ...four legs,

4 ...a tail,

5 ...and a tail club!

Tail club

20

6 Now draw in three rows of jagged spines along Ankylosaurus's back.

Draw in his
eye, mouth, and
three horns.

Color in with
felt-tip pens.

21

Spinosaurus

(spine-oh-sore-us)

1 A Spinosaurus needs a body,

2 ...a head and neck,

3 ...two legs,

4 ...two arms and hands,

5 ...a tail,

Sail

6 ...and a great big sail!

Kentrosaurus

(Ken-troh-sore-us)

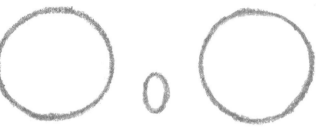 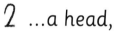 

1 A Kentrosaurus needs a body,

2 ...a head,

3 ...a neck,

4 ...four stumpy legs,

5 ...and a tail!

6 Now draw in a row of spikes from his neck to his tail.

Draw in
Kentrosaurus's
eyes, nose,
and mouth.

Draw in one long
spike on his shoulder.

Color in with
felt-tip pens.

25

Velociraptor

(Vel-oss-ee-rap-tor)

1 A Velociraptor needs a head,

2 ...a body,

3 ...a neck,

4 ...two legs and feet,

5 ...a long tail,

6 ...and two arms and hands!

Draw in Velociraptor's eye and nose. Add big sharp teeth.

Draw in a huge claw on each foot!

Color in with felt-tip pens.

27

Plesiosaurus

(Plee-si-oh-sore-us)

1 A Plesiosaurus needs a body,

2 ...a long neck,

3 ...a little head,

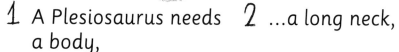

4 ...two front flippers,

5 ...two back flippers,

6 ...and a tail!

28

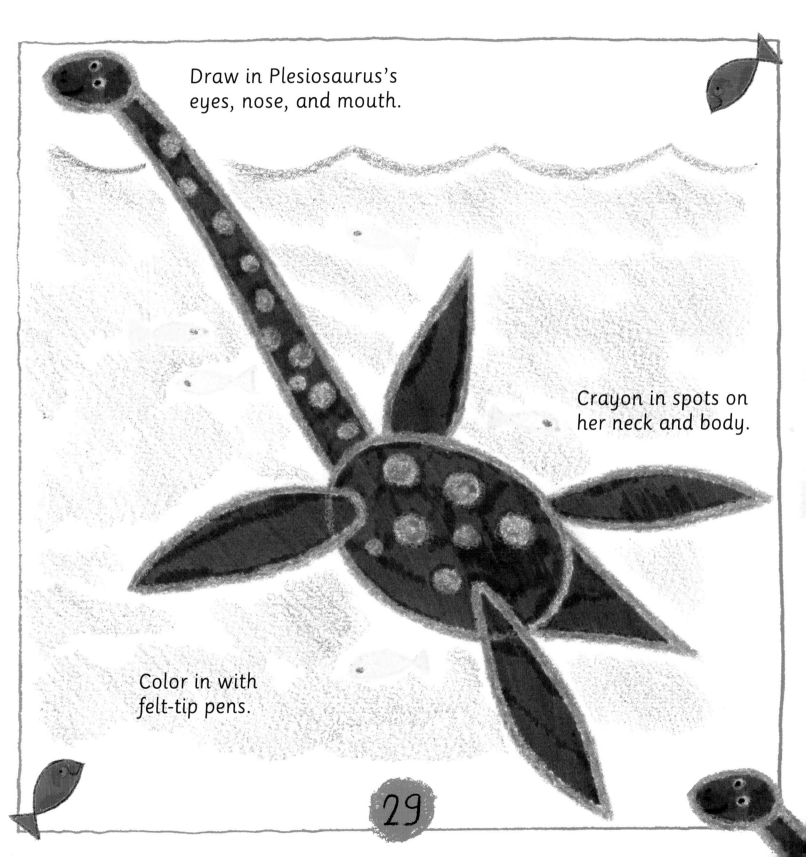

Draw in Plesiosaurus's eyes, nose, and mouth.

Crayon in spots on her neck and body.

Color in with felt-tip pens.

29

Pteranodon

(Pter-an-oh-don)

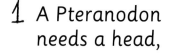

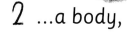

1 A Pteranodon needs a head,

2 ...a body,

3 ...a neck,

4 ...two legs and toes,

5 ...two big wings,

6 ...and two arms with fingers!

Draw in Pteranodon's
eye and mouth!

Draw a zigzag pattern
on her wings.

Color in with
felt-tip pens.

Glossary

Beak a hard, strong, and sharp mouth without teeth, used for tearing food and for defense.

Eye ridge a lump of bone above a dinosaur's eye.

Flipper the wide flat limb used for swimming by an animal that lives in the sea.

Head crest an oddly shaped bone on a dinosaur's head.

Neck frill a large flat piece of bone attached to dinosaur's neck.

Sail a large, thin hump on a dinosaur's back, held up by long bones.

Snout the part of an animal's head containing the nose and jaws.

Tail club a lump of bone at the end of a dinosaur's tail, used for defense.

Thumb spike a sharp, pointed claw on the end of a dinosaur's thumb, used for defense.

Index